A Mother by the Window

A Mother by the Window

KAPIL RAJ

Anecdote
Publishing House

Anecdote Publishing House
E-35-A, E Block, Gali No. 2, Ganesh Nagar,
Pandav Nagar Complex, Delhi - 110092

Published by Anecdote Publishing House
Copyright © Kapil Raj

First Edition 2023

ISBN: 9788195890743

MRP: ₹ 149.00

All Rights Reserved.
No part of this publication may be reproduced, stored, in
a retrieval system, or transmitted in any form, or by any
means — electronic, mechanical, photocopying, recording or
otherwise — without the prior permission of the publisher.
Opinions expressed in it are the author's own. The publisher
is in no way responsible for them.

Book Promoted and Marketed by Champ Readers Pvt. Ltd.

Layout and Cover by Anecdote
Printed in India

*To all the free souls,
hurt, chained, and caged
by social rules and
fabrications*

Change Stories by
Kapil Raj

Change Stories by Kapil Raj is an amalgamation of five independent short stories: **Kuroopa, A Gutterful Life, First Love Many Times, Flying with Chains, and A Mother By The Window.**

Advancement of humankind invariably poses new challenges to the existing social order in society. It weakens the bondages enforced by patriarchal rules, paving the way for societal awakening. However, every ounce of progress leaves behind some debris in its wake. Failure to recognise this debris or 'problem' can bestow acute misery and suffering in the lives of people. Going back and snipping the problem in the bud is usually more cumbersome than revolting and moving forward.

If only there was an easy way out.

True social development cannot be achieved without breaking existing stereotypes and adapting our mindsets to the subsequent changes.

Each short story interweaves a heartening story with a deeply imbibed social issue, hardened public belief, and associated fabrications. As you read the narrative, you watch and evolve with the characters, sometimes feeling yourself in them – empathising in circumstances that may or may not have existed in your lives. The stories will highlight the suffering that was never supposed to take place had we brought about a meaningful change for ourselves and others in the society.

However, there's always a first, and it can start here.

We live how we think, and we think how we choose to live.
Progress is hard; change is heroic.

Acknowledgements

Every beginning has a story. We often emphasise too much on the journey and the end goal, forgetting all about that *first step*.

When I commenced writing *ENDURER A Rape Story*, I was scared spending nights on the outcome. From the inception of the idea to getting the story published, three years passed. The book finally, reached the hands of readers and found love in a way I had never imagined.

For the first time, when I held the mic in a room full of young students to speak on the subject (rape and sexual assaults) which is considered one of the biggest taboo in the Indian households, my hands trembled, yet I took that leap.

By the end of each of session, I was gifted emotions, witnessed appreciation and respect. It was a dream come true. But a thought lingered behind. What next? What topic should I pick? Will I be able to justify the appreciation and recognition I received? The turmoil was too much. For a moment, I felt giving up. In those times, there are people who stand with you, influencing in ways which do not let yourself stop and take on unfamiliar paths.

They are my parents, my wife Payal, my sister Dimple and my son Hetarth. I owe you.

Pulkit, Thank You. You always stood along. When I simply could not progress further, your faith in me made me hold on and continue to move.

Tatiana, I am grateful for your persuasion and astute conversations. You incepted ideas on which I was able to write and build these stories.

Tina, you have my gratitude. You chiselled out the entire work with your editing and added a clear voice to the words.

Sincere thanks to Anecdote Publishers & Sagar Azad, who trusted me with my unconventional project and extended all support to get published.

And most importantly, I would like to thank all my readers. Your reviews, personal texts, praises and critiques motivated me to walk through this journey.

1

2 Likes and 10 Views.

Neetu refreshed her Instagram profile repeatedly. After four hours since the upload, the counter trudged to mere twelve views. It appeared to have given up and died after that. 'This is what you deserve!' said a robotic voice in her head. She scrolled over to Aisha's account, who had also just posted a video. It had only been a few minutes and her views were over a thousand.

Neetu had picked a song after days of research. She had gone through hundreds of Reels to learn how to lip-sync with ease and then practised them herself, with many attempts saved in draft. After finishing her daily chores, she set her hair, applied makeup, and wore a fashionable dress to style her look for Instagram. There was a corner in her house with great lighting and a backdrop of plants. She recorded her video there, lip-syncing over a popular song. Satisfied that the video was exactly how she wanted it to be, she uploaded it with the trendiest hashtags and a caption titled 'Feeling myself.' The entire process was quite enjoyable. However, the lack of responses and engagement on her post nullified the efforts and disappointed her. Neetu refreshed her account again. The counter was still the same. She threw her phone aside and dropped onto her bed, drained and dejected.

"Mom, what's for lunch?"

Neetu jumped out of bed when she heard Rahul's voice. The children were back from school. She couldn't believe that four hours had gone by just to make one Reel.

"You promised fruit custard today!" screamed Rahul, finding an empty freezer and a clean kitchen slab with no visible signs of progress. Neetu rushed towards the kitchen and grabbed some fruits from the refrigerator. In haste, a few pieces tumbled out of her arms and fell on the floor, some rolling under the kitchen sink.

"Dimple, can you please pick them up?" said Neetu.

Dimple, an obedient child, heard her mother and jumped off the sofa to come to her aid. However, in her excitement to aid, she failed to notice a puddle of water on the floor – the water camper was leaking. Dimple slipped, lost her balance, and fell on the floor like a soft toy. The only difference was the loud cry that followed after. Neetu left her station and rushed to help her daughter, consoling her with a bunch of kisses.

"What is this ruckus?" asked Ammaji, entering the scene and taking her seat at the dining table. To her amazement, all the serving bowls were empty. She noticed a grumpy Rahul, a weeping Dimple, a clean pressure cooker, and several uncut vegetables and fruits. Ammaji's eyes spread wide open with disbelief.

"Neetu, what is all this?"

Irritated out of her wits, Neetu carried Dimple in her arms and handed her to Ammaji without replying, silently asking for support. Then she hurried back to the kitchen to make pulao – a quick rice dish that always comes in handy in case of emergencies.

Ammaji calmed Dimple in a few minutes, but her amazement was not over.

"Neetu, what have you been doing since morning? Why isn't lunch ready yet?"

The words pierced Neetu's heart, but she continued to work in silence, trying to focus on the task at hand. What is the worst thing to happen in life – to be answerable to others for something as basic as a little personal time.

2

Neetu finished all the afternoon chores, such as making lunch, washing dishes, etc., avoided Ammaji, and then locked herself in her room with a small cup of tea. She glanced at her image in the mirror. The clothes were trying to hide an unfit body. The complexion fading due to inattentiveness. The reflection resembled nothing like the memory of herself when she had dreams and aspirations – which she had to give up in order to take care of her family. It's a sacrifice that is seldom remembered or appreciated, as it's part of the 'compromise' that every girl has to endure when moving into a new family. Marry for life security and then thrash all hopes of having a career to care for your children and in-laws. Neetu was constantly reminded by Ammaji that there were women who worked but still had to take care of their family – basically Neetu was lucky. Go figure!

It was not that Neetu was unhappy, but you can't measure success in life by happiness alone. She had no meaning, no purpose, no fulfilment of her existence. She opened the drawer of her nightstand and pulled out a picture of herself. It was when she won Miss Meerut's title during her college days. She had so many desires, roads to take, choices to make, but alas! A teardrop fell on the photograph. Aisha was always jealous of the attention Neetu received from the opposite sex, a feeling that had led to the culmination of their friendship for some time.

Neetu's marriage to Govind was quite hurried. He belonged to a wealthy business class family with no demands for dowry. Her mother refused to listen to anyone and decided Neetu's fate for her. A day after the last college examination, she was forcibly dressed and made to walk down the aisle to accept a future that was not of her choice.

Today, Aisha had more than 25K followers on Instagram. She worked in a bank and had married a co-worker. She chose not to have kids and was an influencer on several social media platforms. When Neetu last met her, she was told that Aisha received several products for free as a part of brand marketing. Even her gym membership was free since she regularly promoted it online by posting exercise videos and tagging the place.

Unlike Aisha, Neetu was not jealous of her friend's success. She felt something – perhaps strange unease, but it was nothing negative, like jealousy or hatred. Neetu was rather helpless in this regard and was unable to ignore the comparison with her best friend. She would spend hours looking at Aisha's photos and videos, reading her comments to see how she responded to her haters and their trolls. Before she knew it, the subconscious comparison had taken over her conscious mind and she couldn't get this topic out of her head. From Aisha, she would divert her attention to other women who had achieved similar levels of popularity at their age. Neetu would observe the smallest of details, then compare herself with the photographs while looking at her reflection in a mirror. All this led to a simple conclusion – if Aisha can do this, why can't I?

Neetu rechecked her Instagram. She had managed to scavenge two more likes, including one from Aisha.

"So! My heroine has also entered the field," said Aisha on the phone.

"Yes, make fun of me," replied Neetu, trying her best to hide her frustration.

"It's not easy. I know this. There is a lot of planning, focus and constant thought that goes behind creating new content. You have to understand dynamics, ask viewers, socialise, have suitable clothes, try something new, and be open to experimenting with your appearance. I mean, this is just the tip of the iceberg."

"I get all that," said Neetu, clueless in reality.

"Start small, lose some weight, get better clothes, step out a little, and spend some time watching Reels online. Most importantly, get a better smartphone and ask your hubby to start taking your pictures as a new hobby!"

"Does everybody need to work so hard at this?"

"Neetu, these social media platforms are the new

rage. We need to start from somewhere to make our presence felt. Otherwise, be happy with friend requests from aunts and good morning messages from uncles."

3

Neetu was never an early bird, but familial responsibilities compelled her to change her habits. Someone once told her that a girl sleeps until she is married, then spends the rest of her life paying back for the luxury. She had smirked when she first heard this, but now understood the harsh reality. She usually woke up at five to start with the daily chores. That day she left bed at four in the morning.

While brushing, she heard Ammaji snoring. The noise crafted a spell of hypnotic sleep, and her head dropped twice, but she managed to stay awake. After changing her clothes, she walked to a nearby park. Different age groups greeted her with a smile along the way – these people were of two kinds. One said 'for how long can you come to the park?' and another insinuated 'welcome to the sleepless society.'

Neetu briskly walked, jogged, and also joined the ongoing yoga group. She returned home by the time she usually woke up every morning. No wonder it was a new experience. As she shook her kids and woke them up for school, the warm, cosy air in the bedroom enticed her to go back to bed. It was beckoning her to give in to the sensation of sweet slumber but that was impossible.

Neetu sent her kids to school with packed breakfast and lunch, gave Ammaji her tea with medicines, and handed over the newspaper to Govind. She still had fifteen minutes left before progressing to the next task of brooming and mopping the floor. During this time, she played some of the cardio videos she had saved and tried to exercise. She was out of breath in under five minutes. For a moment, she felt like a monkey could perform better than her. Well, she knew her body had become too stiff over time.

After serving lunch to Govind in the afternoon, Neetu bid him adieu as he left for work. Ammaji was satisfied with her stew and had no complaints. So, Neetu took some time to explore more Reels and realised she needed a lot of new photographs for her profile to begin with. She had started to look older than her age.

She wondered if Govind would help her, but he had not been himself lately. His elder brothers had shamelessly hijacked the family business after their father's death. Influenced by their wives, they sent Ammaji to live with him so they could be free of the burden. Govind, an immensely principled man, stood his ground and tolerated his family's drama with his head held high. He started a construction firm with his savings and received investments from the city's wealthiest people due to his father's reputation. Despite his success, this entire process had taken a toll on him, resulting in zero interaction with his wife and almost little to no time for his immediate family.

Neetu understood all of this, but still she had to convince Govind to go out for dinner. Her main agenda was to get some good pictures clicked with great backdrops outside their home. She could have gone with her neighbours Juhi or Prachi, but they were both terrible at taking photographs. There was a time when Govind wanted to become a photographer. Now all of his equipment had been sold for the business.

After working all day, Govind returned at six in the evening. Neetu asked him if they could have tea in their room. Surprised by this unusual request, Govind nodded and silently moved to the bedroom. He settled on the bed and started scrutinising some contractor documents.

"I was thinking," said Neetu, placing two cups of tea and a plate of salted biscuits on a tray beside the bed. "It has been very long since the kids have gone out..."

"I don't have time," responded Govind without shifting his gaze from the documents.

She placed her hands on the papers and gently lowered them.

"Then make some time. It has been months since the kids have stepped out anywhere with you. Yes, a lot is going on, but they have not forgotten the old times."

Govind was clearly getting irritated, but he

listened to Neetu patiently.

"That new mall nearby. Let's go there after dinner. Just ice cream, so nothing expensive."

Neetu's thoughtfulness convinced Govind. Women always found their way, he thought. There was a twinge of shame as his family had to undergo such hardship because of his misfortune. He smiled, agreeing with his wife. Neetu was overjoyed with the results of her little play. Her mind had already wandered to the dress and hairstyle she'd donned that day.

4

Neetu kick-started the dinner preparations. While the dal was in the cooker and a curry in the pan, she quickly ironed the kids' clothes. Rushing back to prepare rice and roti, she instructed Rahul and Dimple to finish their homework quickly. Rahul was stupefied to see his mother hurrying about, juggling so many tasks at once. Neetu emptied the food into big bowls on one hand and rummaged for a piece of jewellery on the other. They were going to the mall – the woman could not slow down. There was a time when they would spend an entire day outside, starting with a movie in the afternoon, followed by a leisurely lunch at a restaurant. The excitement would ebb onto a gaming parlour, and depending on their energy; they would dine at Govind's favourite restaurant or get the food packed. Neetu did explain to her children the dire financial situation they were in. Despite his young age, she expected Rahul to act like a responsible son and a sensitive brother to young Dimple. He was unable to join the school picnic due to the high fee and felt embarrassed among his friends. He understood all of this and yet loathed their circumstances. Why didn't his dad take his rightful share in the family business?

His mother had berated him for behaving poorly, but he felt no shame. All his friends had a new gadget or technology to play with – iPhone, PlayStation or Netflix subscription. They had something to enjoy. He didn't even have a decent phone to play a few games on; the phone would keep getting stuck, accelerating his fury. His mother disappointed him. Why did she have to include him in her plan of savings? He was only fifteen years old; it was his time to enjoy new things and experience life. His father had no time for him and his mother always said 'no' to each request. He was one of the few kids who still went to school on a bicycle – all his friends rode bikes or scooters.

So when he heard about the plan to have an early dinner and go to the mall for just ice cream, he was infuriated. What kind of stupidity was that? Why this formality? He scolded Dimple, who was hopping all over the house in excitement. But his words had no impact on her. She glided across the house like a fairy without wings, fuelled by her happiness.

Unable to concentrate on his homework, Rahul screamed at Dimple to keep quiet. The impromptu scream startled her, and she jumped, losing her balance and falling on the floor. The best she could do was hold on to something before ramming into the chair. What she grabbed was the tablecloth, which came down along with a jug full of water, spoons, a few utensils and a plate of salad. The crash and the subsequent cry echoed throughout the house. Neetu came running in her new salwar suit to witness the horror.

She panicked; this scene meant half an hour of additional cleaning. Dimple tried to explain the situation through her sobs, pointing at her older brother while she did. Neetu's eyes filled with anger.

"He made me fall," said Dimple.

Rahul, anticipating an explosion, opened his mouth to explain, but before he could utter a single word, Neetu slapped him right across the face.

Reeling with shock, he yelled, "I don't want to go

anywhere!" and ran to his room, hiding his tears. Neetu bent down to pick the pieces of broken glass and almost got stuck in her fitted dress. She cleaned everything with a broom and cleaning cloth, trying to prevent sweat from ruining her look. Govind would be home in twenty minutes. She restored everything as fast as possible and changed Dimple's water-drenched frock.

Rahul observed from his window, rubbing his hand over his burning cheek. Usually, dad went on a frenzy; mom never lost her cool. There was a strange zeal in her actions today. Despite being so uncomfortable in her dress, she still magically cleared all the clutter. He almost saw tears in her eyes when she realised all her efforts in getting Dimple dressed had gone to waste. However, she had brought everything back to normal in a few minutes. He was still trying to understand the urgency of this visit and now, being a little afraid, changed his clothes silently and waited for his dad.

5

After dinner, the family left for the mall in their old car – a gift from Govind's dad. The non-functioning AC and the humid air melted the layers of artificial beauty from Neetu's face. She was aware of this, and before a complete wipe-out, managed to take some selfies with Dimple in her lap. Rahul shifted towards the window to get away from the frame.

They parked their car and entered the mall. The

entire area was littered with fancy stalls. People browsed through the products of their desires, which invariably disappeared after glancing at their price tags.

'Everything in the mall is so overpriced.' If Rahul heard this one more time from his mother today, he would have to answer back. He was frustrated about suddenly being deprived of all the leisure he enjoyed during his grandfather's time. But his mother seemed a little different today. She window-shopped with eyes full of desire. Her pace reduced to such a level that Govind and Rahul had to frequently wait for her. Neetu would catch up after languidly admiring a dress, a jewel, some footwear or a handicraft item. Then she would take selfies as if making a diary.

Govind started to feel a little uncomfortable. His understanding and caring wife seemed to be taunting the things he could not afford. He remained silent and questioned his thoughts. The ice cream parlour was on the third floor. After taking the escalator to a particular level, they had to walk through shops to get to the next, taking in the view of some more dazzling stores. It was as if a monster was hidden in the walls, luring ordinary people into emptying their pockets.

After reaching the parlour, Govind ordered strawberry ice cream for Dimple, a chocolate one for Rahul, and mango flavoured one for himself and his wife. Neetu took pictures of the ice-creams, herself, Dimple, and then invited Govind to join her.

"How are your studies?" Govind asked Rahul, ignoring Neetu's request.

"Good, exams are almost near, dad." replied Rahul, surprised. His father had inquired about his studies after a long time.

Neetu was busy looking at her pictures. Most of

them were blurry. She looked fat in a few, and if there was a decent click photo, it was being photobombed by either Dimple or random strangers moving about in the mall. Her excitement was slowly ebbing and getting replaced by irritation.

"What is funny with you?" asked Govind.

"Nothing," replied Neetu.

"Can't you leave the phone and just enjoy the moment for a while?"

Neetu relented and kept the phone down. She was pretty dispirited as she licked the last few mouthfuls of her dripping ice cream. After finishing her cup, Dimple screamed excitedly and leapt away, inviting Neetu for a chasing game. Neetu sighed and fulfilled her wish. At the same time, Govind sat beside Rahul and chatted with him for a long time.

When they returned to their car, Neetu asked Rahul to take her picture next to a designer tree. Rahul obliged but did it half-heartedly. Still not impressed, she finally asked Govind to take one decent photo of her.

"Where has this new obsession of taking pictures come from?" shouted Govind, with no sense of keeping his voice down. Neetu gulped with embarrassment but maintained her composure.

He went back a few paces and clicked a series of photographs on his phone. Neetu did not dare ask Govind to show her the pictures instantly. She waited to reach home, changed her clothes, prepared the bed, gave almond milk to everyone, and then politely requested Govind to share the pictures with her. She anticipated and received a few grumbles, along with the photos. She looked at them and was relieved to find them satisfactory. Her outing was finally successful.

6

Neetu surfed through tons of photo editing applications. She installed and deleted them after realising they were no good. If she managed to like the result of one, the application would not allow her to save without paying. That was cheating, she thought. But she did not stop and finally discovered one with decent output. After that, she copied suitable captions and popular hashtags from another application that suggested maximum engagement and finally posted the pictures. This was the result:

15 Likes, 4 Comments.

Neetu did not lose hope. She had all the qualities to become an influencer. She researched and continued reading articles to learn how to increase her fan following. Not only would it benefit her financially, as she had heard. But most importantly, it would give her satisfaction, a sense of achievement. If Aisha and hundreds of women could do it, then she could too. She was not allowed a career, a job, or even a business, but no one could take this away from her.

She delved deeper into the analysis. Many times, she literally wracked her head as to why a certain video got a million views. She hated those accounts that used skin-show as bait for getting more engagement. She was sad to see that boys and girls in the name of 'my life, my choice' promoted that ideology. Hours of scrolling started to affect her daily schedule of work.

She was constantly thinking of original ideas and began posting every day – pictures and videos of home-cooked meals, decorated temple area inside her house, morning walks, rising sun, blooming flowers, feeding dogs, festival celebrations, etc. Despite all this, she failed to cross a hundred followers by the end of two months.

#

Part of being old is to notice the inconsistencies around you. People think that the aged have lost their minds, but in actuality, they see everything. Their experience can deduce trouble much before it appears. Ammaji knew something was going on in Neetu's life. Her daughter-in-law gets up early than the usual time, leaves the house for a walk in the park, forgets to add correct spices in food, and burnt rotis. She had even started to avoid her favourite serial in the afternoon and seemed lost all the time. These were only a few of the observations that Ammaji had recorded in her mental diary. Occasionally, she would hear music from Neetu's room at odd hours, or see a freshly scrubbed face after removing makeup right in the middle of the day. Each activity was completed in haste or delayed some important household work. The common element to all this chaos was the phone in Neetu's hand.

Ammaji kept quiet for a few days, but when Neetu forgot to add almonds and walnuts in Govind's milk three nights in a row, a mother had to take her stand – not literally. Ammaji had great difficulty in standing up; she could just about manage to do her personal chores every morning.

At night, the new Neetu quickly served food on the dining table. She cleaned the kitchen, emptied the garbage, boiled the milk, and left for the bedroom. Govind washed his face, changed his clothes, and quietly had dinner while watching TV. In his mind, he appreciated how efficient Neetu had become. The table seemed decorated to him. There was a covered tumbler of water and a glass of milk next to his food. Also, a small towel hung on the right side of his chair to wipe hands. He touched the glass of milk and found that its temperature was perfect. He kept his food aside and raised the glass to drink.

When he gulped the first sip without chewing anything, Ammaji knew that Neetu had forgotten to add dry fruits in the milk again. She waited for him to finish drinking and then called him out.

"Yes, ma," said Govind, sitting down next to his mother, thinking of the many bills and accounts he had to settle for the day.

"After him, you have taken a lot on your shoulders. I can ask uncle…" said Ammaji, teary-eyed.

"Ma, let us not discuss this for the hundredth time. I am trying to stand on my feet."

"Your father raised his children to be strong, but I guess only you learned from him."

"Ma, go to sleep and please don't overthink," said Govind, almost getting up.

"I know you have a lot on your plate, Govind but as a father and husband, you have other responsibilities too."

"And am I not fulfilling them?" questioned Govind, taken aback by his mother's words.

"Spend some time at home; notice what's going on. Something is not right."

"What do you mean? Tell me. Is Rahul getting out of hand, or did Neetu say something?"

"I won't say another word. I don't want to become the cause of a fight between husband and wife." When parents say these words, they are fully responsible for what comes after.

"So it's Neetu."

Ammaji remained silent and turned over, leaving Govind in confusion. Within minutes she started to snore – she had relieved the weight from her shoulders after all.

7

Govind was content with Neetu. She never bothered him, and if she did, she would adhere to his wishes silently. He imagined this was the reason he loved her. In his family, men took the household decisions, and women were supposed to follow them. But he was different; he respected her obedience.

Initially, there had been a few quarrels on trivial matters, such as cooking poorly or staying at the office late into the night. But Ammaji and his brothers' wives ensured her training process, like chiselling the sharp edges of a newfound knife. Neetu was always silent but humble in taking the initiative to help others, which he always liked. After his father's death, they were forced to move into a tiny house. Neetu accepted their circumstances and, with limited resources, made the place worth living.

But Ammaji's words created a disturbance in Govind's mind. He was too tired to enquire any further, so he went back to his room and got ready for bed. He had noticed that Neetu was quite charged up as compared to her usual slow self. The messy hair were gone, she seemed more fit, her skin glowed, and she was always engrossed in the phone. Even after lights out, he would notice her tiny phone screen glowing in the dark.

Was this related to what Ammaji was trying to warn him about? He wondered. What would

Neetu do on the phone except watch some series or browse new recipes? He slept, surmising that Ammaji was simply overthinking.

#

Neetu's efforts were in vain. She had applied all the metrics, followed the tutorials, and experimented with content, but the reality was unavoidable. She was a thirty plus woman with no social life where she could have friends to like or share her posts. Her house was in shambles, with no lighting or background for good videos. There was no support from her partner. The husbands of her counterparts were chiselled and well-groomed. Not like her husband, who had no time for anything apart from office work.

Some videos made her laugh, but she could not see sense in most of them. A couple dancing to music where the husband washes utensils gets thousands of likes. People walking in slow motion get millions of likes. Changing clothes on a theme is so popular; what is the obsession with transitions? Was there any meaning to all this? People were dancing to everything. Even while giving medical or financial advice, they would dance, point their fingers in space, and add text later. How do they get the energy or training to do this? She was horrible at it – a corpse could dance better than her.

Failure was imminent, and she was sure to lose her determination when she got an idea – she could get a pet. Yes, videos with cats and dogs received a lot of attention. But getting a pet meant a lot of investment, and clearly, their pocket was tight. Neetu decided to ask Govind, and if he refused, she would insist. For years, he had not given her anything. He had even forgotten her birthday last month. She prepared a speech to convince him and one to confront him if required.

"Can I ask you for something?" said Neetu,

handing over the homemade dessert to Govind.

"Tell me," he said, ingesting a mouthful of kheer. Neetu paused until she noticed the expression of delight on Govind's face after tasting the sweet delicacy.

"Can we have a dog?" she asked with her best smile, fingers crossed behind her back.

Govind paused. The sweetness of the desert mellowed his outburst to an extent.

"… as a pet," she added, being cautious.

"No, we don't need a pet," he said, giving the bowl back and diverting his attention back to his file.

Neetu clenched the bedsheet in anger. She glanced at the floor, which shone in the moonlight, the result of her hard work. She worked all day and night, never raising her head in protest, always accepting things that came her way. Home, children, family – that's all that existed in her life. How easy it was for Govind to refuse her request without even considering her feelings. He did not bother to even look at her before or after the refusal. Her body ached with the day's exertion, her heart with helplessness and dependency.

Tears mixed with the detergent water as Neetu scrubbed the utensils in frustration. She could never master the word 'NO' – it had no meaning in a mother's life. She would receive it time and again, but she was not allowed to use it. Neetu remembered her mother. Even after a day of continuous standing, she would run around the house to clean, panicking if the dal got an extra boil, or the dough became a little fluid. Not knowing how to stop, she would endlessly tolerate her body aches aiming for one thing only – the welfare of her family. And if she ever crashed down, the anxiety that came after was more out of concern for her family than her recovery.

Even in that condition, if dad asked for a glass of water, something that he could easily fetch himself – her face never reacted, but her body did. With the support of the bed, she would force herself to stand up, drag her feet to the kitchen, and fulfil the request while sitting with a thump. That momentary pause would make her close her eyes and take a deep breath. Mentally, mother was screaming 'NO' for any more requests but never used it, nor did anyone hear it.

8

Neetu left the bed at dawn, after tolerating Govind's snores throughout the night. She was extremely enraged. Entangled in disappointment and rage, she slumped on the living room sofa. She tried not to glance at the clock. Even though she was furious and sad, the clock's needles still owned her. With every tick, they nudged her to regain her senses and start doing what she was born to do. Neetu ignored her subconscious and tried to resist, but the worry of her children getting late to school and everybody demanding food engulfed her. Eventually, she got up and lit the stove.

Govind switched off his alarm clock and got up early. He called for his tea and went to take a bath immediately after. It was an important day today; he had a crucial meeting with an investor from Delhi. He had asked Neetu to iron his favourite shirt a few days ago. The shirt had been exceptionally lucky for him many times in the past.

After a hearty breakfast, Govind checked his almirah, but the shirt was nowhere to be found.

"Where is my olive green shirt, Neetu?" he yelled in frustration.

Neetu heard him and came running into the room.

"The shirt, Neetu?"

Trying to remove the fog in her brain, it took

her a while to understand the question. After some thinking, she remembered that it was still in the washer. The anger from the previous night vanished and was replaced with fear. She had never forgotten to complete a chore before. Her eyes skewed, cheeks puffed up, and eyes fluttered about – Govind knew that apologetic face too well. He threw the towel in his hand and was speechless for a moment. He had no words for her negligence.

"Where is your mind these days?" he yelled.

Neetu looked down, owning her big mistake. The kids watched their mother standing like a culprit in front of their father. When Govind lost his temper, he did not care about his surroundings. Rahul understood the situation and interjected an explosion by asking for a plain piece of cloth – it was required as part of a project in school. He emphasised that they were getting late. Neetu escaped the scene and searched for a piece of cloth in the almirah while wiping a tear from her eyes. Apparently, her negligence had deeply hurt Ammaji too. Neetu was sure she would hear incessant taunts about this the whole day – just like a malfunctioning alarm clock without a snooze button.

"Poor Govind, he works so hard. Does he need this extra tension? Such an important day for him, and see how he left the house. I gave that shirt to him after fasting for a full day. He has never failed a task in that shirt. Full one thousand rupees I spent on it." And on she went.

Govind lost the investor. He did not come home for lunch and kept mourning in his office. His expressions revealed the outcome. Everyone at home understood that things had gone south, but nobody dared to ask. Rahul took Dimple into their room and studied quietly. Ammaji paused her radio; she blamed Neetu for this defeat.

Govind dropped onto the bed without saying a word, his clothes and shoes still on. He was devastated. This single investment could have fixed all his petty loan requirements. He had chased the investor for months to get a meeting, and now he had to start again from scratch. Neetu made coffee instead of tea and some fries with it to improve Govind's mood. She slid the tray with caution and sat down next to him.

"God will help us," she said.

"Leave me alone!" The volume of his outburst was a warning for Neetu; she stood up and left the room. Food is the best solution to most problems. Who doesn't like to eat in distress? The unlikely combination of coffee and fries healed Govind momentarily, and he got up after emitting a huge sigh. The way is long and full of hurdles, but that defines the road to success. He ignited his motivation by remembering the past and his brothers' humiliation. He repeated the thought while allowing himself to rest for a day and start afresh tomorrow. While browsing for headache medicine in the drawer, he found a letter with a bank logo on the envelope. He tore it open and read the contents – it was a query for his application. He noted the date; the letter was received last week.

He screamed, calling for Neetu. She came running back into the room. Glancing at the envelope, she knew it was her mistake, and even worse was the timing at which she had been called out – she was dead frightened.

"Enough is enough, Neetu. What is wrong with you?"

"I… I am sorry."

"No, you have to tell me what's going on! All this exercise, training to become some heroine, wanting a dog. Is there something you should be telling me?"

"Govind, please calm down. The kids are still awake."

"Stop turning this on me! You asked for this. You have one little job, one! Manage this house and family."

Little job? The words clanked and thundered in her head. She spent her entire day and part of the night working tirelessly for her family. That was little? And why did she do it? Yes, making food was her responsibility, but mostly because nobody else could do it and they were too poor to hire a cook. But none of her neighbours walked the extra mile to keep their house clean, like Neetu did. She extracted ghee from milk at home. Instead of buying packaged condiments, she ground whole spices with her own hands. The list was endless, but apparently all her additional efforts, commitment and love for the family were just a job for the people around her.

Govind noticed that her phone constantly pinged with notifications. He took it from across the bed and unlocked the screen. His expressions became angrier with every finger scroll.

"Have you lost your mind and standards? Don't you have any shame? Vomiting your life on Instagram! Really? Getting lewd messages from unknown people for a private shoot?"

"Govind, I am an educated woman. They are probably spammers."

"How can you defend yourself like this? You are enacting these third-class videos. What if my brothers saw it? Don't you care about our family's name? What will *Chachaji* think of your photos? This shameless dancing. What are you getting out of this? Where is your self-respect? Now I understand why you were behaving so weirdly in the mall."

Neetu felt a twinge of fury underneath all the numbness and fear. She had never reacted to Govind's outbursts. But this time, it was as if he had pushed her to another level, where there was no understanding and no respect for each other's feelings. It was as if she was living with the illusion of a husband who was nothing but a stranger in reality. The threads had come undone.

"What family Govind! The one who expelled their brother for money? You know what is third-class – this house and the conditions we live in. Are you worried about Chachaji? Let me remind you that he happily accepted my jewellery in return for settling your petty loan, which ideally he should have paid on your behalf, and you think you are a son to him? All your brothers refused to keep their beloved mother with them. Please explain to me how your family name or pride has been maintained by these acts?"

Govind was shocked. The heat of the argument, the coldness of her expressions, bewildered him. This was Neetu, his wife, the person he had lived with for over a decade. Today, she had broken the threads of reliability and become what he had never imagined her to be. Gradually grasping the truth of her words, he could bring himself to accept defeat in front of her. He flung Neetu's phone across the room, crashing the device after it stuck the window.

Govind clutched her arm and forcibly pulled her face towards his. She screamed in pain.

"Shut your mouth. Your mind is corrupted; you are not Neetu!" he said and left, aggressively pushing her aside.

9

Bits of glass and plastic lay scattered on the floor. Neetu had always wondered what a shattered heart was; those broken pieces seemed to represent this age-old metaphor to her. In her imagination, she always felt relieved after confronting Govind. But in reality, she was riddled with guilt. Why?

No matter what intellectuals claim, celebrities or movies represent, society has reserved an inferior place for women – that is the ground reality.

Their existence depends on a simple theory – get married and raise a family. Don't speak, express, or try to feel anything – just follow the drill. The forms might change, a few definitions might get altered, but the definition of a 'good woman' or a 'respectable woman' remained the same. Even if she won a gold medal in the Olympics, her life would depend on the same conditions. Privileged are those who can escape social stigmas and claim their life as their own.

Neetu understood her mistake. Once married, she did not exist. She had to adhere to the rules made by society for a mother, a daughter-in-law, or a wife. In truth, men are not responsible for this mindset at all – it is actually cemented and accepted by women themselves since birth. For her pain today, her mother, the wives of Govind's brothers, Ammaji, they were all responsible. Things are equally bad for men; she won't deny that. There is a considerable weight of responsibility and painless masculinity that is expected of them, but they still have a pinch of freedom. Women are told to be proud of just being their support system.

The day Neetu got married, she boxed her dreams and aspirations in the hope of reliving them someday. In reality, she should have killed them then and there – there was no hope for married women. Yes, it is a pity. Millions of women work incredibly hard to gain some presence on social media. Their goals might be different, but she knew hers clearly. It was a platform where she could grow as a person and maybe get some small benefits or recognition in the future. She took out a photo concealed in the depths of one of her books. Her eyes misted over as her brain took a trip down the memory lane. Cameras flashing, the din of clapping hands, the interview, the coverage in the newspaper – everything flashed through her mind. She was still very proud of that day. Neetu recalled winning the Miss Meerut competition and suddenly, in the blink of an eye, tore the picture into a thousand pieces as if to erase that memory forever.

Govind never left home late in the evening. His disgruntled appearance and angry demeanour that night might become part of the neighbourhood gossip. Neetu wiped her tears and picked up her shattered phone. The screen had frozen; there was no way she could use it to make a call. She sighed deeply and dialled Govind's number from the landline. He picked up the phone after a couple of tries.

"I am sorry. Please come home. You mean everything to us. We all depend on you. My outburst was temporary. I just got carried away," said Neetu mechanically. She knew the words had to be said, whether she felt them or not. This is what a loyal wife was trained to do. Govind disconnected after hearing her words. A final lesson for her, she thought. A woman's happiness resides outside herself, in places defined by society.

#

Rahul heard everything. His father did not lower his volume for the benefit of his children. He marched out after having a row with his mother. Rahul witnessed his mother taking a stand for herself for the first time, and he appreciated it. Every word she uttered was true and reflected his feelings too – dad simply did not listen. Surreptitiously, he slid into his parent's room to comfort his mother, but she was not there. Whenever mom was sad, she would walk on the terrace for hours – he knew where she was.

He noticed the broken phone and picked it up. A few notifications from Instagram were frozen on the screen. Rebooting the phone did not work. He came back to his room, searched for his mother's account and browsed through her feed on his phone. There was some serious effort on photo editing, caption writing and hashtags. Pictures of family, videos on the latest trends like 'show you are a mom without telling you are a mom' etc., were worth appreciating.

The account was a few months old. While her initial posts screamed of newbie mistakes, it was clear that she was improving gradually. He could see it was not a personal account and that the hashtags aimed at creating engagement, but she was failing at it. Now he understood her frustration and why she was acting out. The worst part was, dad had broken her phone! Overwhelmed by her innocence, he felt miserable as a son. He should have helped her. No wonder she was not able to concentrate properly. For her, it would have been such a struggle.

Mom loved lemonade with extra honey. Rahul prepared the beverage and took it to her. She was sitting on the raised brick platform on the terrace. Hearing footsteps, Neetu wiped her tears quickly. She was surprised to see Rahul walk in with a glass in his hand. He sat beside her and gave her the lemonade. This simple act of concern broke her resolve, and she burst into tears.

"What? What did I do?" asked Rahul, alarmed.

"You are too young to act like an adult." He wiped her tears and lay on her lap, hugging her.

"I love you, mom. You are the best." He closed his eyes and acknowledged her efforts for the family. She needed some support, and he was determined to give it to her.

10

Neetu woke up without an alarm but did not leave the bed. She had become habitual to her new routine. Birds chirped outside the window, egging her to go for a walk in the park. She decided to ignore them. She had accepted the inevitable fate of an Indian woman – anything for self was meaningless. Maybe she was too selfish to spend significant time on her goal. She could have found new recipes, finished her 'pro level' cleaning, or gossiped with Ammaji. Maybe she was being too hopeful – time was an opportunity, and hers' had gone by. Aisha probably worked her way out of this quagmire at the right time. She maintained everything, house aesthetics, a good understanding with her husband, her physique, every little detail. That day when she looked at the mirror, Neetu lowered her eyes.

After spending the entire day rearranging wardrobes and hunting for insects, she sat down for a while and watched her serial, chopping spinach side by side. Her eyes were blank; she felt empty. A void had been created which her dream once filled. Though seated next to a window, she felt suffocated and wanted to scream. To quell her distress, she found more work – rearranging cabinets, cleaning the washrooms, washing the balconies. Still, the sense of failure did not leave her.

Rahul watched his mother gradually succumbing to her failure. Dad gave him money to get the phone repaired. Luckily, the damage was external and there was no data loss. The first thing Neetu did with the repaired phone was to delete all her posts. This satisfied Govind to a great extent. Deeply hurt by Neetu's rebellion, he chose to remain angry. But it was not easy to ignore her years of dedication. Her action of deleting pictures and videos was in line with his definition of an obedient, loving wife. That day he went to the older part of the city and brought some rasgullas for her – her favourite sweet dish. He also noticed that Neetu was trying to be her usual self. She would promptly respond to his requests and work harder than before. Every day she cooked a variety of dishes, but something about her actions seemed forced. Like she was dispensing every ounce of her energy so that eventually nothing was left inside.

#

It was a holiday, and after having a heavy lunch

of chole-bhature and lassi, everyone felt lazy. Govind watched television with his eyes half shut, and Rahul sat beside him, half-heartedly reading his English book. Neetu still had her cupboard to clean. She took out all her clothes and arranged them in the balcony to air dry. She replaced the old, smelly newspapers in drawers with fresh ones and added some naphthalene balls. Then she took the last carton of her artworks and brought it to the yard. Her hands trembled as she took out one of the books.

It was a book of her paintings. She flicked through them and became incredibly nostalgic. Whether it was a leaf wafting in the rain, doves flying in the sky, or a specially-abled person dreaming about dancing – most of her art centred around the theme of 'escape'. Neetu was reluctant to paint again. Before marriage, her mom made her join cooking classes instead of art, which she loved doing. She still learned the craft all by herself. After marriage, she would paint when she felt low. With time, that escape became a rarity. Even though Govind liked her art and asked her to continue, there is a difference between saying and supporting.

Attracted by the flash of colours, Rahul left his spot and sat beside Neetu, gawking at the beauty of the artworks. He was looking at his mother's collection of sketches, oil and water paintings for the first time. His mind worked as he skimmed through the magnificent pieces. While Neetu was changing the pale covers of the books, she was struck by an inspiration. She picked up a blank canvas and closed her eyes for a while. And like splashing a dream in the real world, she outlined a few strokes. Rahul was spellbound to see his mother bring a blank canvas to life in a matter of minutes. He was taking pictures of her artworks but switched to video mode when Neetu picked the canvas and closed her eyes.

Eventually, she kept the canvas aside and continued to finish her chores. She felt a little better after that exercise. After tea, she sat down in the evening to work on the painting again. By now Rahul could identify the protagonist of the artwork – it was a lady standing next to a window. She had a cup of tea in her hand and was looking out, watching the tall buildings.

Interestingly, along with the structures, there were some mountains and disco lights. The concept pretty amused him. After finishing all the activities, Neetu picked up her colours and began filling in the painting. With each fill, her imagination drew closer to reality. Though in the literal sense, it was still a dream. She was that lady, a mother. The window represented her boundaries, beyond which lay a world that she could watch from a distance but never experience.

A week passed by. She would colour for a few minutes and then get busy again. Some days she had more time to paint. By the end of the week, when she finally finished her masterpiece, she kept down her brush and stood back – a tear dropped from her eyes. Dimple started clapping, and Rahul praised her work by clicking pictures and taking videos with all his heart. Even Govind joined the merriment and appreciated this unexpected piece of art.

#

Neetu liked the rain when she was young. Whenever dark clouds gathered in the salutation of an imminent storm, she would leave everything and rush towards the street. The air would fill with moisture, pushing the dryness away. The first few drops would feel like the climax of a movie; in no way could she guess when they would fall. And once they did, she would clap, jump, and even dance with other kids from the neighbourhood.

After some years, she rode a bicycle in the rain for the first time; it was one of her sweetest memories growing up. But with age, this luxury only rested with the boys, and she was only allowed to watch from a distance – at max, dip her hand in falling water. She silently accepted her fate and learned to be satisfied.

Neetu noticed it was about to rain that day. She went to the terrace and picked up all the clothes before they got wet. The rain meant extra work – crispy pakoras in snacks, cleaning the muddy footprints that people left behind when walking in from outside and waiting for the day to clear so she could dry the clothes again. Did she forget anything? Yes, massaging Ammaji's knees.

"Mom, sit here," said Rahul, gently pressing her shoulders.

"What is it, Rahul? It could rain anytime! I have a lot of work to do," said Neetu, looking at the sky. "Open the photo gallery and the first video."

Seeing the excitement on Rahul's face, she

decided to oblige. It was a timeline video of her finishing the painting from a blank canvas to the final outcome.

"Nice," replied Neetu, trying not to feel too happy about it.

"Open Instagram," said Rahul.

It was Rahul's phone, but there was a profile by her name. The notifications from this account were full of likes, followers and shares. She opened the account and saw that Rahul had been posting her work regularly. The timeline video she just saw was uploaded on Reels. It had gained a lot of attention – thousands of views, likes, and many comments appreciating her work. Neetu was overwhelmed; she had questions and needed an explanation.

Rahul smiled and explained everything to her.

"I took some help from my friends. They all posted this video in their stories and the Reel became featured by chance."

Rahul had replicated her portfolio of artworks. All the other posts were also receiving a lot of engagement. The number of likes were in the hundreds. Most of the videos were creatively edited, something she had no knowledge about. She was dumbfounded when Rahul asked her to check the messages. A lady had enquired if she was interested in selling her latest painting.

Neetu's hand shook, and she gave the phone back to Rahul. She lowered her gaze and spoke with a trembling voice.

"Is she a real person?"

"Yes mom, she is my friend's mother," Rahul excitedly replied. "I cross-checked and she is interested."

The contained and suffocated drops left their abode and dove towards freedom. They might not be in a better place, but they would be free for some time and then demolish their existence. The effort was still worth it; not everyone could understand the pain of captivity. She was still figuring out how to react but there was a smile somewhere deep in her heart, and she knew it was better to conceal it. Raindrops fell at her feet as she stepped into the yard. She tilted her head and felt the rain on her face after many years. Her eyes leaked tears of happiness that immediately merged with her surroundings. They were all free. They existed, even if only for a few moments.

Change Stories – Next Reads

Kuroopa

'Why did God make me so ugly? Am I not your daughter? Was I exchanged at the hospital? Or did you leave me in the sun one day and that's why I became so dark?'

Meera, one of three siblings, has been struggling with her identity since childhood. She is subjected to mean, insensitive remarks by neighbours, relatives, and random people around her due to the lack of pleasing physical attributes. Constant comparison with her fair, blue-eyed sister further deteriorates her relationship with friends, family, and most importantly, herself.

A shocking incident involving the household pets pushes Meera over the edge, forcing her parents, especially her father, to take action and bring her back to reality.

Will Meera be able to find her footing in this hypocritical world that preaches "looks don't matter" while constantly objectifying and running towards beautification? Will she be able to accept herself for who she is and overcome the hatred she has for herself?

A Gutterful Life

Hindus and Muslims live in harmony across an open gutter (naala) at the edge of the city.

Whether it's the story of Somu and Aklaq – two innocent souls from different religions who stumble into each other on the naala and foster a friendship like no other; Billu and Arif – two budding businessmen trying to make a living – who are subjected to inter-community politics through the tryst of fate; or the community's favourite Chai-Chachu – an old tea-seller with unknown origin but an important story to tell, *A Gutterful Life* brings forth a plethora of sentiments culminating in an emotional climax.

Will Aklaq and Somu's friendship survive the vagaries of communal division? Will Chai-Chachu be able to bridge the gap between Hindus and Muslims across the naala? Will religious propaganda compel people to forget their hardships and sow seeds of division in the illusion of unity?

First Love Many Times

'She is my life; she is my love. What will I do if I fail? True love only happens once in a lifetime.'

Abhi falls head-over-heels in love with Kavya at first sight. They become friends and everything is beautiful as if they were destined to be together. Until the day Abhi confesses his love for her at the Taj Mahal.

Catastrophe befalls and Abhi's dream shatters. Completely heartbroken, Abhi decides to fight for his love one last time, like the ones shown in movies. If successful, life would be beautiful again, else he would have to end his life.

Will Abhi be able to understand the difference between true love and the one displayed on screen? Will he see reason beyond his anguish? Does love truly happen just once?

This short story debates the question about first love and the trials and tribulations one goes through to achieve it.

Flying With Chains

Three friends – Yatin, Taruni, and Kunal – have been joined at the hip since childhood. They live close by, go to the same school, and always hang out at the same rendezvous. As they grow up, their parents become uncomfortable about their closeness and try to keep them apart.

Whether it's Yatin's struggle to clear the civil services examination, Kunal's difficulty in convincing his businessman father to let him pursue physics, or Taruni's rebellion to break free from the shackles of patriarchy, undue expectations from friends and family builds the pressure on this trio.

Will their friendship withstand the test of time or will the demands of society unravel their relationship and lead to mistrust and betrayal? Will they be able to chase their dreams or will they succumb to their inevitable fate?

Also by

Kapil Raj

𝒩ow, a national bestseller.

Life was a fun fed roller coaster: new found love, drugs, cat-fights, patch ups, crushes, night hangouts, and unplanned trips. Like any girl, not in the wildest dream, palak could imagine that after attending a rave party, she will wake up to the horror of finding herself raped.

In traumatic conditions and struggle between sanity and hallucinations, she is compelled by the circumstances to leave her world. Already fighting a war within, her stances take a toll witnessing horrifying tales of women and girls. Little did she know that this catastrophe was not enough for one lifetime, and a storm — was just cooling its heels.

Will she be able to carve her path while facing the rapists, her tyrant father, appearances of her passed away mother? Should palak let her life to be decided by people, society, and taboos? Would justice return her life or revenge lend her peace?

A heart-rending story of a girl, whose beliefs and honor has been battered, stands up to make choices, rediscovering the meaning of life.

About the Author

Kapil Raj is a professional, speaker and writer-activist based in Delhi-NCR, India. With the heart of a philosopher, mind of a realist, and a deep-rooted non-conformist, he lives many lives, yet stealing the time for the most precious thing that matters to him: crafting plots, playing with characters, and weaving the stories based on intricate social subjects and challenging the dogmas.

His debut novel *ENDURER A Rape Story* is critically acclaimed by the media and loved by the readers. He is a noted speaker and delivered lectures in prestigious institutions and colleges.

Connect with him on Facebook, Twitter, Instagram @ikapilraj